HOKSILA
and the
RED BUFFALO

by Moses Nelson Big Crow

''Hoksila and the Red Buffalo''
is a sequel to the book
''A Legend From Crazy Horse Clan''

Cover Artist
Dean Zephier, Yankton Sioux
Illustrations By
Bernard W. Provencial, Rosebud Sioux

Tipi Press
Chamberlain, South Dakota 57326

AUTHOR'S NOTE

The story "Hoksila and the Red Buffalo", is one of the oldest stories I know of. It was passed down from generation to generation, like from Grandfather to Grandson. The story changes with each generation.

The significance of it is, as it goes through ages is, it has no horses in it. Only in the "vision quest" parts. The story has to be very old. But like all legends, it keeps in tune with the passing of time. I hope you enjoy it like my Grandfather, me, my children, and my Grandchildren did. Hoka-hai.

Pela-maya-yelo

Moses Nelson Big Crow

ISBN 1-877976-02-4
Copyright © 1991 by Tipi Press
First Printing
All Rights Reserved
Printed in the United States of America

ACKNOWLEDGMENTS

Henry Nelson Big Crow—Grandfather who told me the story
Albert White Hat—helped me with bilingual
P.R. Gregg—encourager, helper, friend
Sinte Gleska College—where I learned bilingual
Bro. David Nagel—who saw the value of the legend
Bro. Ed Bausell—spiritual brother, encourager
Renee (Sansom-Flood) Brugier—who inspired me to write the
    stories of my ancestors.

All our Sioux ancestors that left us this beautiful heritage.

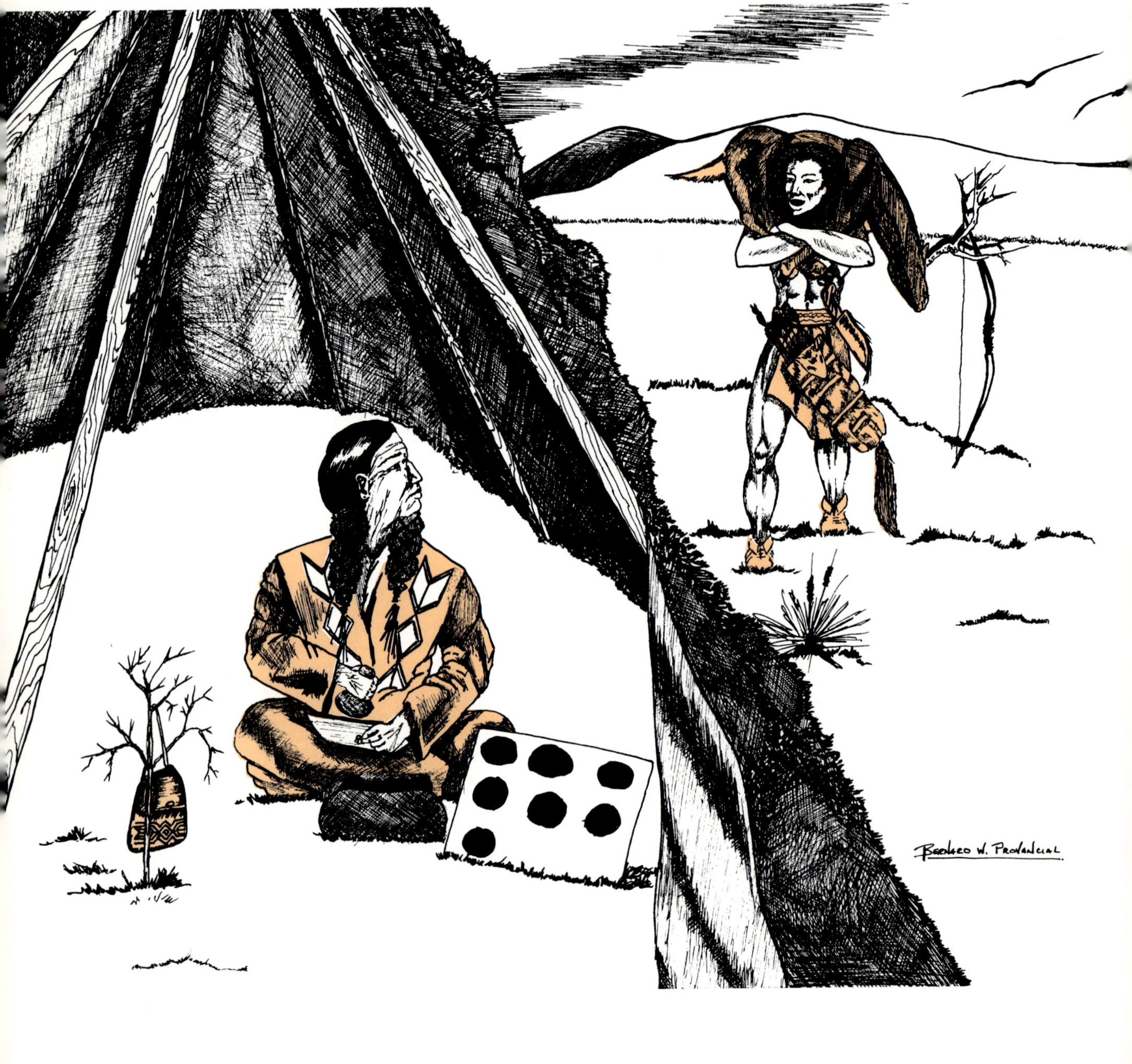

HOKSILA
and the
RED BUFFALO

By
Moses Nelson Big Crow

A young Lakota lad tiredly carried a slain deer on his shoulders as he returned to the tipi where his Grandmother and he lived. He had been raised by this grandmother since his mother left him when he was still a baby.

The story goes that his father had gone on a raid with other warriors and never returned. They brought his packs back though, and told he fought bravely even though they were badly out-numbered and soon chased out of the enemy territory. The young wife of the brave warrior took in all this very sadly. She badly missed her warrior. After that she went off to cry her loss daily, always taking her pet coyote puppy with her. The little coyote puppy would sit and howl when his young mistress cried for her dead warrior.

One day the maiden did not return. In the days that followed, the people worried, finally sending trackers out to look for the grieving maiden. Experienced trackers followed a trail to a large boulder sitting by a river; a smaller rock was beside it. Finally a medicine-man told the people that it was the maiden and her coyote puppy. She had chosen to be there to wait for her warrior husband, and her coyote puppy stayed beside her as always.

The child was left behind with his grandmother. Being a proud grandmother she took it on herself to raise her grandson promising her people that he would hunt and kill the big, ugly, black-spotted, red buffalo that plagued their village and other people. This big, red buffalo with the ugly black spots always killed the young warriors and carried off all the prettiest girls in the villages he raided.

Among these beautiful girls taken was a maiden betrothed to the growing warrior. A grandmother's pride, yet an orphan, the young warrior had no uncles or family warrior to name him, so he was called "Hoksila." He would have to grow up and become a warrior to earn a name. He must also rescue his already chosen wife by killing the great spotted red buffalo that had been holding her captive all these years.

"Ho Unjiji," (Ho Grandmother) the young lad called, "Henapa-yo, Tokcha talo ota awagli yelo." (Come out. I brought back lots of deer meat.)

The grandmother hobbled out of their ragged old tipi and exclaimed. "Ho-hee, ho-hee, takoja, lela washti kshto." (Grandchild, it is really good. Now that you have enough food, and hide enough for another pair of moccasins I will tell you what you must do.)

Hoksila wondered what his grandmother was talking about. She was all he had for a family and he loved her dearly. After the deer was dressed and she had cooked the choice meats for her grandson, she sat him under a shade tree and told him all he was supposed to do as he ate and listened.

She unfolded the story of his warrior father, and the story of his mother who grieved so much for her warrior that the gods turned her and her coyote puppy into stones so they could wait for his father forever. She told him of the red buffalo with the ugly black spots that was always attacking young warriors and stealing the prettiest young maidens. She told him that his chosen wife was among those stolen young maidens held captive somewhere by the beast.

Grandmother also told him she had vowed to raise the young warrior that would hunt and kill this red beast with the ugly black spots so the young people would have no reason to fear again. The invisible warriors of the four winds told her they would help her warrior all they could. She had fasted and prayed for this; they answered and gave her assurance. But first, Hoksila must offer flesh and fast so the warriors of the four winds could contact him, instruct him and give him all the other help they could provide. This was their promise to the grandmother.

When all this was done, then Hoksila would begin his long journey, his hunt to rescue his wife and kill this ugly menace. Then he could free all the young maidens.

For ten days Hoksila prepared. First he looked and found the strong, young cherry tree that would make him a strong bow. It would be the best he ever made. Next he would cut the best red willows to make into fine, straight arrows. He looked again and found a very fine piece of stone. This he made into a strong tomahawk and practiced with it until he could throw it expertly. He could chop with this as well.

At last he was ready. He went to his wise old grandmother and showed her everything he prepared for his journey and hunt. Now he must go to a far mountain top where he could be alone. He must start his fast and pray. The invisible warriors of the four winds would contact him and do as they promised giving him instructions and describing the help they would provide.

He helped his grandmother take down their worn old tipi. Hoksila silently promised himself that his dear old grandmother was going to have a new tipi made from the hide of that red buffalo with the black, ugly spots.

He fitted his shoulders into the loops on the travois poles and moved out. His grandmother had their provisions in the packs on her shoulders and back. They traveled for two days to the high and lonely mountain where the young warrior was to fast and make his contact with the spirits of the four winds. His grandmother had picked this place years earlier.

It was the dawn after they made camp that the wise old woman took her boy warrior to the mountain top to begin his fast. He took all his weapons so the spirits could touch them and put their power and strength on them for his coming battle. Hoksila was going up against a fearsome and formidable foe. He needed all the help the spirits could give him. The grandmother and her warrior knelt and prayed. When the sun threw its first flashes through the skies the old woman left so her grandson could start his prayers and fast. She would wait alone at the bottom of the mountain. The young warrior would return to her on the dawn of the fourth day.

Hoksila knelt, his body bent, his forehead on the ground. He listened, his eyes closed and arms outstretched. He prayed hoping the innocence of being alone and in prayer would encourage the spirits of the four winds to come close. After a long while he heard the grating and scratching sounds of something approaching. Slowly he raised his head and opened his eyes. A very large snake had come to sun itself at the very same spot.

Hoksila looked and asked, "Ho, Tunkasila, le kola ke ay ho wo?" (Ho, Great Father, is this my friend?)

Immediately he heard thunder and a streak of lightning dimmed the mid-day. The big snake coiled itself and raised its head. Lightning sparks danced around the fasting warrior. The big snake made a hasty retreat and was gone.

"I guess he is not my friend," thought Hoksila. "He is not supposed to be here." He smiled as he thought of the frightened big snake.

It was after mid-day when the man came. He was finely dressed in tanned deerskin breechcloth and vest. Everything he wore was done in beautiful beadwork. He carried a water-bag, what his people call "Talaja."

"Hau Kola, lela bluko welo, (Hello, Friend. I am very tired)," he said as he sat down on the edge of the rock.

He jiggled the water bag sloshing the water. "Sne yelo, huk yachi hu wo?" (It is cold. Do you want some?)

Hoksila did not answer. The man drank his water taking big thirsty gulps, and Hoksila could hear the water gurgling in the man's throat. The man finished with an, "AAHH," and smacked his lips. He poured some water in the palms of his hands and washed his face.

"Lela okatay lo, (It is really hot.)" he said.

Soon after he pulled out some papa saka (dried meat strips) and chewed on one. He was making delicious, smacking sounds as he chewed the meat. He took out his big hunting knife. Cutting off a piece, he offered it to Hoksila.

With tears in his eyes the young warrior shook his head.

Just then a young female voice sounded, "Lela okatay kshto, letchiya hu pay. (It is really hot. Come on over here.)"

A beautiful maiden sat in the shade of an upright boulder. Hoksila couldn't take his eyes off the maiden beauty.

"I have come to help you free all those young maidens from the red buffalo with the ugly black spots. But now you must rest so you will be ready to travel and do battle. Do not be afraid. We are here to help you." The beautiful maiden held out her arms to him, "Come I will help you rest." She smiled a beautiful smile for him.

Hoksila moved, then closed his eyes. His grandmother had told him two helpers were going to be sent to him. Were they here? Still, he thought, he had one more day left. The whole day and then the last night. It would be so nice to start his journey and hunt now. He was so hot, thirsty and feverish that he wanted to lay down and rest. The beautiful maiden got up and started toward him. She carried a fine beaver pelt robe.

"Kneel on this, and here is water," she said. She looked to the skies suddenly and said, "You must come with me now, very quickly. A thunderstorm is coming up very fast! Hurry!"

The girl waited. Hoksila opened his eyes to look. He saw low rolling clouds coming toward him. He could see lightning bolts hitting the earth. A big thunderstorm was coming in very fast. The maiden became very excited.

"Come, we must leave now! That storm is very dangerous. We will take shelter under that ledge until it passes. Come, Hoksila!"

She smiled at him invitingly as she reached for his arm, but the thunder interrupted, "Hoksila, ahyushta yo, wechichala hecha shni yelo. (Hoksila, leave it alone, it is not a maiden.) O'waji yaka yo. (Sit still.)"

Hoksila turned his head and saw a meadowlark on a cedar branch.

Again the thunder voice called, "Negna yelo, negna yelo. (It fooled you, it fooled you.) The thunderstorm closed in fast now.

Hoksila looked toward the coming storm. He could see it was a long line of mounted warriors which extended the entire length of the storm front. The hooves of the charging war ponies caused the low rumbling and rolling of the clouds. Every time two ponies touched a lightning flash ignited. War whoops raised the storm to a high pitch.

Suddenly two warriors on spotted ponies charged ahead of the horde of the storm. Was one Hoksila's father and the other his grandfather? The two charging warriors were far apart. Hoksila could see them sign-talking to each other. Then they bent low on their ponies and came charging with lightning flashes everywhere.

As Hoksila watched, the fine pelt the maiden brought him turned into many mice and they all ran off in different directions. The waterbag turned into a turtle and was trying to crawl off the rock. Hoksila

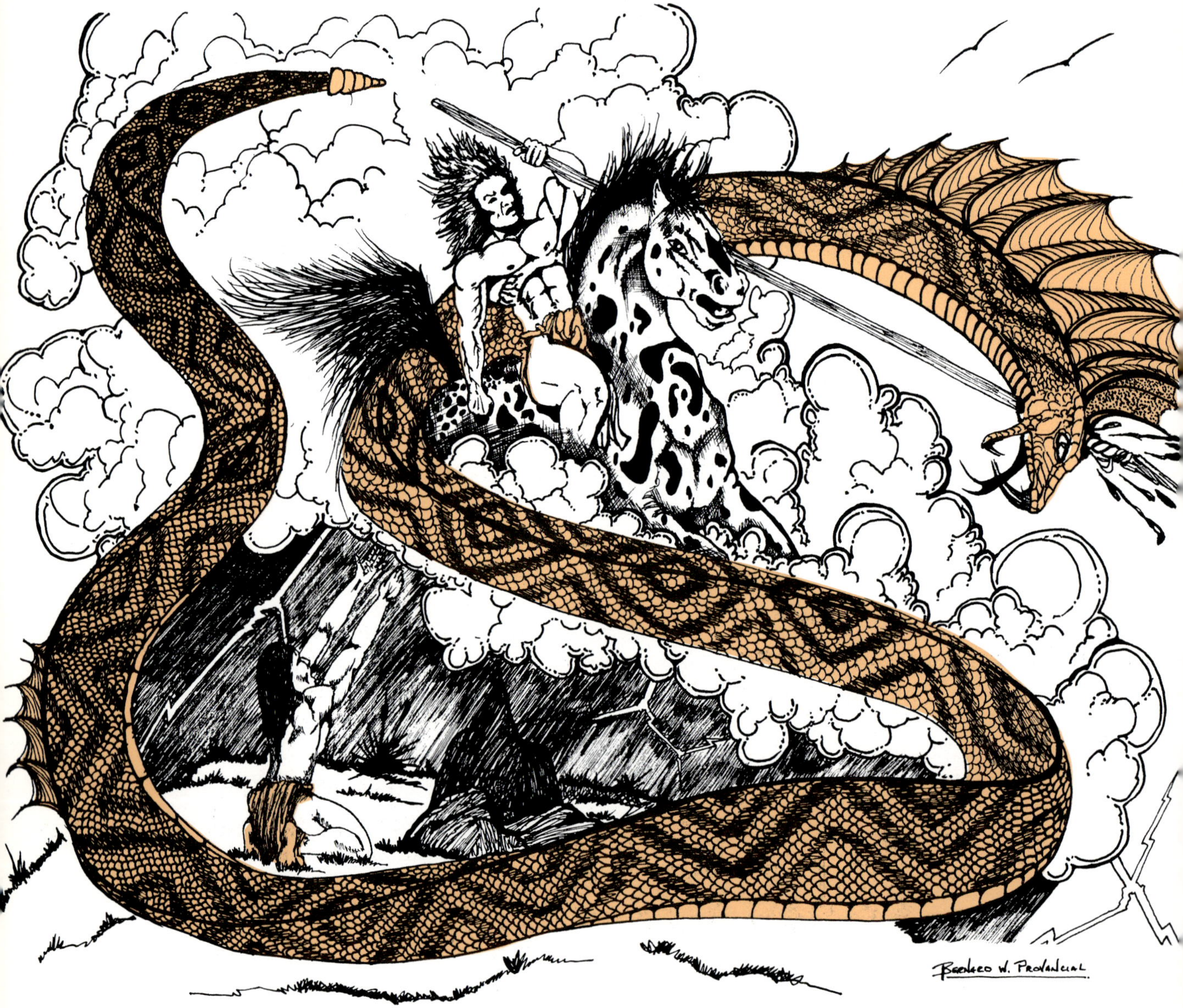

heard a loud hissing. The beautiful maiden had turned into a very large snake and curled itself around the rock Hoksila was praying on. That finely dressed warrior had turned into a snake too, bigger than the one wrapped around Hoksila's rock.

The two snakes raised their heads high and stood coiled to meet the two charging warriors. The bigger male snake shifted to the front while the smaller one held Hoksila prisoner. With tongues flicking out and large fangs snapping, the two giant snakes met the charging warriors. The mountain-top shook and rumbled as the two warriors slammed into the giant snakes. Flashes and sparks were everywhere. Huge boulders were flying in all directions.

The two warriors made their pass and moved on. Behind them a long string of charging warriors was following them in. Each took a chunk out of the huge first snake as they passed by. The big snake's screaming was soon just a low moan as the warriors cut it to pieces. As Hoksila looked back, the first two warriors were returning. Now they wanted the snake surrounding the fasting warrior.

All the other warriors were now galloping their horses in a circle so the last snake wouldn't escape. Now it was surrounded.

The snake lowered its head and spoke to Hoksila in desperation, "Hoksila, please tell your father and grandfather to let me live. I will turn back into that girl you loved so much and serve you for the rest of my life. I will give you something to keep forever."

Hoksila couldn't answer. He was still in shock. At the last minute the snake struck out at him. A rider with a spear in hand mounted on a spotted horse crashed in between them impaling the snake through the head. Still holding the spear, the rider pulled the snake after him as he rode up high above the thunderhead and other clouds. There he released the snake and let it crash back to earth. Hoksila came out of his shock and knelt in prayer to give thanks for being helped in a very close call.

The rider came back from the thunderstorm and stopped his horse close.

He announced, "Tomorrow you serve your last day. Then a spirit will come to you and tell you what you must do. Pray well. You have much to do. Pray so you live to do all this. Hoka-hai."

The rider turned his horse and disappeared back into the raging storm. Hoksila wondered what else was in store for him until the morrow. Just then the meadowlark appeared.

"Unjiji tun yunkay lo, Unjiji tun yunkay lo, (Your grandmother is doing fine.)," it announced.

Hoksila turned around, raised both hands in the air and prayed. His fast continued. Soon it was evening, then darkness. It was all peace and quiet into the night. Soon the sun made dawn and wanted to appear. He stood and greeted the rising sun, the beginning of his last day and night. He must now know who his helpers are, then rest and start his long-awaited journey. He may never return and only his dear grandmother would miss him.

He laid his weapons in front of him, took out a root of Sinkpaytawoti, chewed it and started his prayer:

"Ho Tunkasila, na katuya topa ke. . .(Ho Greatfather and the four winds.) I am humble, I have nothing but myself. I am lonely for my wife who is held prisoner by this most feared creature in the land, the red buffalo with the big black ugly spots. I want to slay this beast and take my wife home to her people. This I vow I will do. He will have to destroy me to stop me.

"I want to slay him. This I must do so all the young people will never be afraid again. And my dear little Unjiji needs a tipi. It will keep her warm in the winters. All this I vow I will do. . .Ho Tunkasila, hetchel wachi yelo. . .(Ho, Greatfather, all this I want.) I beg you, give me the strength, the wisdom, the guidance, and the courage to do this for my people. Give me the two Makochi wamakoshkun (two earth creatures) to help me do this. . .Pela maya lo Tunkasila. . .Thank you Greatfather."

Hoksila bent, resting his hands on his knees. He cleared his throat. Straightening up, he sang:

"Tunkasila unshi mala yo-wani ktacha letchamo yelo heya, haya."

Both hands raised and looking up he danced, and sang to the sun. It was early morning, the foggy haze from the hidden mountain springs was visible. A meadowlark woke up and picked up the chant to help. Little tree birds flocked to the singing and picked up the rhythm. Young coyotes chorused in the distance. The mountain-top became enchanted.

Too soon the burning sun positioned itself to mid-day. The little tree birds sang from the shadows of the tree leaves. Now. . .older coyotes joined with their throaty howling. It was eerie, despite the day.

Hoksila's throat was dry, and his knees and ankles ached. As he stood, sang and danced, he heard the clatter of hooves. He could hear the grunts of running animals. As he sang and danced he steadily watched the sun. Suddenly, a great herd of buffalo were running across the sun. They blocked the sun's light and all was dark. Then he didn't know anything, but simply felt the relaxation of his aching muscles and a quiet comfort.

In a loud voice came, "Hoksila, kikta yo. (Hoksila, wake up.)"

He woke up on the flat rock he was still laying and fasting on. Above him stood a tall, handsome warrior splendidly dressed in fine tanned leathers and the most beautiful beadwork Hoksila had ever seen. The warrior carried no weapons. A full-grown coyote stood rubbing against his beaded left legging. A meadowlark was on his left shoulder.

The warrior reached down and helped Hoksila to his feet.

"Letcha cha yachi whoa, (Is this what you want?)," the warrior asked and pointed.

All the mountains were gone. All Hoksila could see was the open prairie and a small lake. All along the shores of the lake he could see beautiful young maidens washing their feet or just swimming. Above them on a knoll stood a huge red buffalo with the ugly black spots. Its beady black eyes stood out in the red-haired face. The tail tip was black.

Unjiji (Grandmother) will have a nice tipi, thought Hoksila. He was looking at a huge ugly beast.

The warrior spoke, breaking Hoksila's thoughts.

"Remember the hill with the twin peaks. Remember that rock ledge on the left peak. That will be on your right because you will be coming from the other side of that. I will give you three more arrowheads because you will need all three to kill that spotted red buffalo. When you come, steal your wife and lure the red buffalo away so all the young women can escape and go back to their families.

"You must fight, run, hide, then fight again. That buffalo herd is all his family. They will try and kill you and your wife. You must be

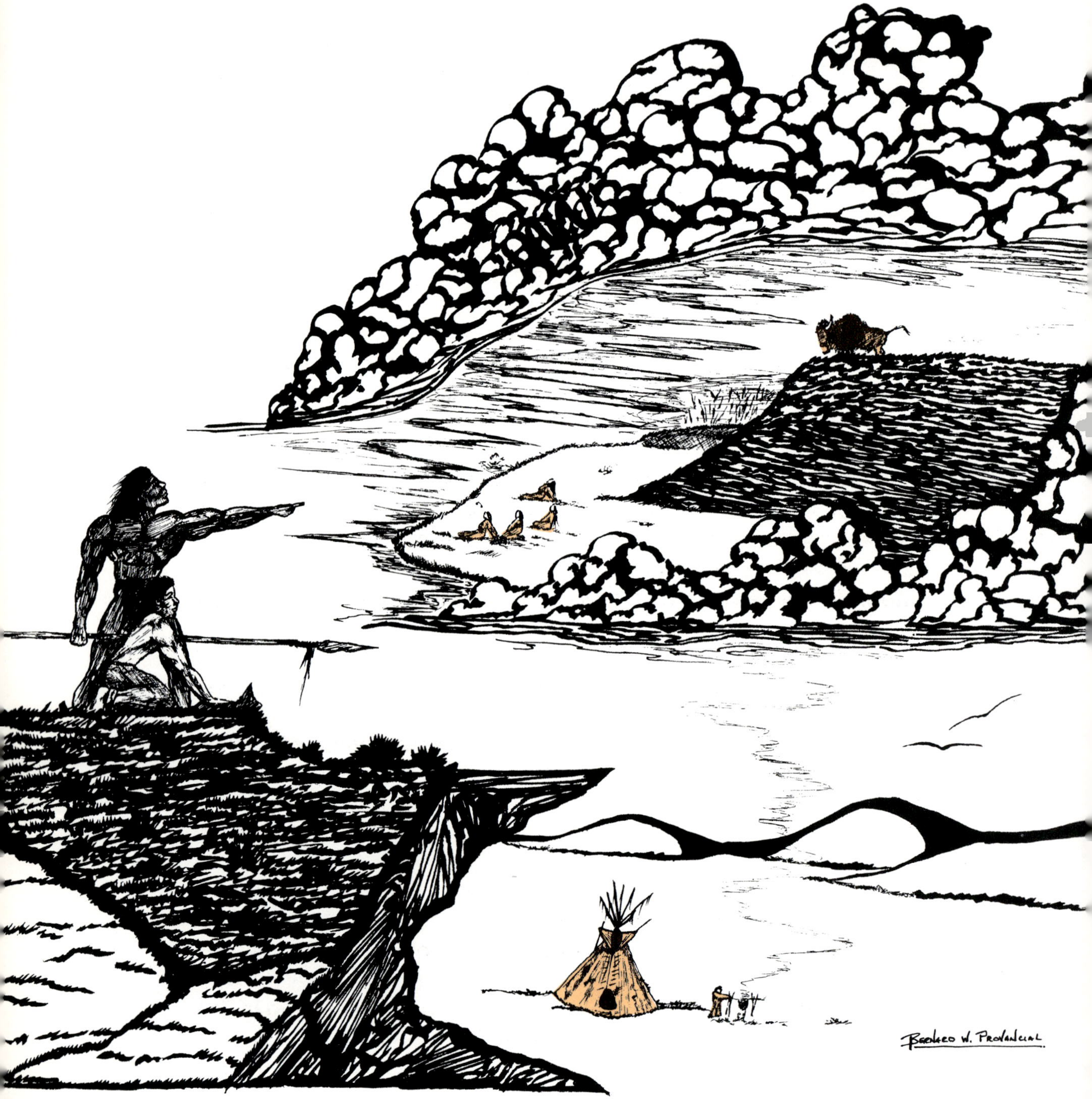

clever. That big red buffalo is clever too. He will not rest until you are dead and your wife is his again. Never forget he has a very large family.

"Here is the help you were promised. This Tashia-gnupa (meadowlark) has many friends across the lands. They like to talk. They will tell you what you need to know every day. They will tell you how to get to the hill with the twin peaks. Don't forget the one with the rock ledge. You will watch the red buffalo and his herd from there. You will know when to go in and steal your wife. She knows you and she will be waiting."

Hoksila was shocked by this last bit of news. She knew him and she would be waiting?

Hoksila was taken aback by this news and a lump filled his throat and tears almost formed in his eyes. He was glad he was dried out from his fast. Now he must really go after her and take her home to his grandmother where she would be safe. Yes, that big hide would also go back for her tipi.

The warrior broke his thoughts as he spoke again, "Next I will give you this Shung-monitu, the Mashlay, (Coyote the clever). Your last gift. He can smell water, the buffalo and other animals. He knows the wilderness. He knows many hiding places—places the buffalo or you never knew. He will be your scout and guide. He will watch for you at night and guide you by day.

"Now you must go to your grandmother. She has prepared food for your journey. Take the arrows and the food, start your journey, you have much to do."

Hoksila looked to the young maidens and wondered which one was his wife. He turned to ask the warrior but the warrior was no longer there. Only the coyote was standing there beside him. Suddenly he felt very chilly and drowsy. He fought with all his might as darkness fell over him.

The chill made him shiver and shake. He finally opened his eyes. He was still on the mountain-top and it was still dark. He turned on his left shoulder and saw the morning star. Slowly, everything he saw and was told came back to him. Then he realized he had a dream or a vision. He was gone a half day and all night. Did he actually go to see the spotted red buffalo and the imprisoned maidens? He knew now he must go to his grandmother. Strangely, he felt well rested and was not at all hungry.

The sun threw daylight into the skies and onto the earth. On the horizon it was taking its first peek, the shield of the lone warrior coming to see his people. He was starting his long walk to the next horizon.

Hoksila raised his hands and prayed. He gathered his weapons and started walking down the mountainside to his Grandmother's tipi. The tree birds were cheering and singing to the sun as it rose higher and higher. The hidden mountain springs were chasing the fog from their clear waters.

Hoksila smelled the delicious smell of boiling meat as he neared the tipi. He wondered how his grandmother got meat. Maybe she went buffalo hunting while he was fasting he thought. He smiled as he pictured his old grandmother hunting buffalo. The buffalo meat soup had cooled, and the meat had been pulled out for eating. A small fire heated more rocks. The tripe was heated again. Grandmother was glad to see Hoksila finish his fast.

After a hearty meal Hoksila was ready to begin his journey. His grandmother prepared him with all the things he was told he needed. As he headed out in the open plains he heard a coyote howl. His scout was telling him which way to go. He turned and waved a good-bye to his grandmother. She waved back with a big smile.

Hoksila felt good as he walked towards the coyote waiting on the knoll. When he got there the coyote was already trotting in the direction he must follow. Hoksila was in good physical shape for a journey like this. A revenge song his grandmother had taught him came to his mind and trotting he sang:

"E'hani letchamu-kta cha-o'yog washi kunm tokay oyakap shni yalakaya, (I said I was going to do this, I told them to tell, I guess they didn't tell) ah hey yo hey yo."

He chanted this song over and over as he trotted after the shung-monitu to the eto-kaga takia (south). It was past wecho kun heya (midday) when his coyote guide suddenly slowed down and walked warily around some commotion in the grass.

Hoksila ran up close to see what was going on. Suddenly he saw the snake, a very large prairie bull-snake busy trying to catch a bird. The bird was a waki-yela (turtledove) with an injured wing. It kept fly-hopping around and the snake was amusing itself by chasing it before it easily caught it and had a delicious meal. It was a sickening sight. The boy warrior raged in his heart as he watched this. Then he crouched low with both arms spread out, quietly closing in on the snake. The big snake turned its head just as Hoksila grabbed it around the neck. The snake had been too busy enjoying itself before its meal; now it was too late.

It was very strong but Hoksila was too angry to notice as he applied all his strength in his grip around the snake's neck. The shung-monitu took the waki-yela in the safety of his mouth and carried it a short distance to guard it. From there the two creatures watched as Hoksila and the big snake grappled. The snake had its long large body wrapped around Hoksila's arm but Hoksila was strong too. Soon the snake was limp. In the warrior's hand was the crushed head of the snake. Hoksila let out a mighty war-whoop and threw the dead snake up in the air. Then he went to check the injuries of the waki-yela. Shung-monitu, the moshlay was still guarding the bird. Hoksila checked thoroughly but nothing was broken. The bird was just badly mauled by the snake's teeth.

Hoksila went back to where the fight had taken place and he raged all over again. He found broken pieces of blue shells, the color of the eggs these birds laid. The Waki-yela had been defending her nest and eggs but the big snake had easily chased her out and ate her eggs. He thought of his grandmother when he saw this. She would have done the same thing the turtledove did. His dear grandmother would have fought to the death to save her grandchild. He let out a shrill yell as he raged.

Then he thought of that red buffalo with the big ugly black spots. He vowed he was going to kill that ugly beast and make a tipi out of its hide for his dear old grandmother. Now he must be on his way, but first . . . Pulling out his big hunting knife he went to the snake. He skinned it around its mouth and jaw, then taking a firm hold of all this he peeled the skin off all the way to its tail. Holding the skin up in the air he yelled, "Hoka hai tatank gleshka hehan neya yelo, (Spotted buffalo, you are next)." His hair on his left side always hindered him when he aimed his arrow so he gathered it in a bunch and tied it down with his new snake skin. Now he could see a lot better with the hair out of the way.

He inspected the Waki-yela closely and knew it couldn't fly. It would be helpless on the ground. He cradled it to his chest and called, ''Ho Kola, wanna eya yo, (Ho friend, go now).''

Hoksila, the Shung-monitu, and the Waki-yela resumed their planned travel at a trot. The sun was merciless but the boy-warrior had his mind made up. Inviting water was sloshing in the water-bag dangling from his waist strap. The wounded bird hugged to his sweating chest. He followed the coyote at a trot chanting his revenge song. Soon the sun was setting on the horizon. The coyote turned into a deep draw never slowing his pace. Before Hoksila followed his guide into the draw he noticed a herd of buffalo in the distance. He was being deliberately led out of sight.

After a long while they came out again into the open flats. Hoksila spotted a flat-top long butte. His guide headed toward this particular butte. When they reached the top, Hoksila stopped to find a comfortable sleeping place and checked his surroundings. He fed his guide and the wounded bird. Taking the roots from his pouch he doctored the wounded bird the best he could. He stood and gazed at the open countryside. He felt very small. It seemed like the flat of the prairie kept rolling until it met the sky.

Hoksila wondered which way they would be traveling. This was a very big land he thought. When in his vision the warrior had shown him the scenery he forgot to check the position of the sun. In fact, he never even saw the sun. He wondered at this.

He laid down on a grass patch. He put his food and water bags under his head. He saw the coyote gently playing with the Waki-yela as he went to sleep. He was tired. He dreamed. The same warrior that came to him on the mountain-top was here again.

''Hai Hoksila.'' he greeted. ''One more day and you will see the twin peaks I showed you. But I must tell you, that certain buffalo you are hunting has been warned. The noisy Unkchi-kika (magpie) that feeds on the lice on the buffalo's back has carried the message to the red buffalo with the ugly black spots. Even now he has scouts that are out looking for you. The bis-bisa (prairie dogs) will remain quiet as you pass their villages. The birds will not fly off in alarm at your approach. The deer will not be afraid of you.

"The prairie snake and the noisy Unkchi-kika are your enemies. You have a very valuable friend in the Waki-yela. She has powers that will help you survive and fight that dreaded red buffalo. Don't forget you have to fight the whole family, and they are many. I will talk to you only one more time before you meet your enemy. The powers of the four winds are with you. Plan and fight well. Free all the young maidens. Hoka hai!''

The early dawn chill woke Hoksila. Meadowlarks were calling messages to each other, exchanging the latest news. In an instant they were announcing, "Hoksila wana kikta yelo, Hoksila wana kikta yelo, (Hoksila is awake now, Hoksila is awake now.)"

The sleepy boy warrior got up and picked up the injured bird to inspect its wounds. It was healing fast, and should be able to fly very soon. It cooed a cheerful "thank you" as he set it down. He fed his scout, then laid out some offerings for the wandering spirits of warriors long gone. Lastly, he sat and ate the wasni (mashed berries) his dear grandmother prepared for his trip. He ate leisurely as the sun tried to appear. When the sun did come out, he got up. He stood with both hands raised as the shining shield of the walking warrior brought light to the land. He called, "Ho Tunkasila, na zuya wicasa, (Ho Tunkasila and the warrior). Give me a good day as I near my destination—the twin peaks. I will honor the spotted red buffalo with those big ugly black spots as I slay him and take his hide for my unjiji's tipi. Unshi mala na umpetu washti maku wo, (Pity me and give me a good day). Hoka hai, pela maya yelo, (Hoka hai, thank you)."

He gathered all his weapons, tying everything to its place on his waist strap and carrying pack. Picking up the injured bird, he pressed it to his cheek and told it, "Toku kia washtay ktelo, Waki-yela, (Everything will be fine turtledove.).

To the coyote he called, "Hoka hai kola, wakul unyum ktelo, eya yo, (Hoka hai, friend. We are going hunting. Go now!)"

They came off the butte and continued their journey. After an uneventful morning of steady trotting they climbed a hill and stopped to rest. Hoksila put the injured bird on the grass and sat down. The coyote found a certain point on the hill and started barking in a new direction.

Hoksila went to the coyote to see what was wrong. He looked in the direction the animal was facing. In the far distance he saw the twin peaks barely above the haze. His heart jumped at the sight of this. He smiled for soon he would see his wife. His waiting was now coming to a close. He wondered what she looked like and laughed. He started back to his packs. The injured bird was fly-hopping, chasing and catching grasshoppers. Hoksila was glad to see this. He was told the bird could help him.

They rested and after a long thought, Hoksila called the Shungmonitu and told him, "When the sun is on the horizon we will be at the twin-peaks. I have sinew and must make three arrows. I will need magaksecha weyaka (duck feathers) and a wood of the Choppa's (beaver) dwelling. They will still be wet and heavy. I must have strong heavy arrows. Take us to a place where I can get these before we reach the twin peaks. Hoka hai."

Gathering his packs and weapons, he picked up the bird and followed the coyote off the hill. They started traveling in draws and gullies. The waki-yela would leave Hoksila's hand and fly a short distance ahead. Hoksila would laughingly pick it up and encourage it to try some more. Soon they came into a wooded area with a stream. The coyote traveled upstream as if looking for a place to cross.

Suddenly it stopped and stood very still. Hoksila dropped to the ground and slowly peeked out over the tall grass. Ahead was a beaver dam, complete with the beaver den structure. Just what he needed. He got up and started walking along the water's edge toward the wood structured beaver's den.

"This is what we will do even before the sun sinks to the hills," he announced his plans to the two earth creatures. Then Hoksila picked bunches of sage. He soaked all this in the water then called the coyote over to him. He took the sage and rubbed the coyote thoroughly. A buffalo cannot see far but it can smell. He didn't worry about his scout being seen. This is Shung-monitu the Moshli, Coyote the Clever, he thought. "Eya yo kola, (Go now, friend) and find out where this ugly thing is and if the maidens are still there. We will travel slow to the twin peaks. Please return unharmed. Hoka hai."

The coyote sniffed the air, stretched out, then headed out for the twin peaks at a run. He would find out everything Hoksila wanted to know. Now Hoksila held open palms to each side of his mouth and called, "Ho Tashia-gnupa, wachiche yelo, ekta ma-u-wo, (Ho meadowlark, I need your help now. Come to me.)."

He could easily talk to these birds and he needed them now. In a little while he heard one.

"Ho Kola, wachiyung wa he yelo, toka huo, (Ho friend, I've come to see you. What is wrong?)" It was a male meadowlark asking questions.

Just then another meadowlark spoke out. It chirped, "Hu hu hee, Hoksila etcha he kshto, (Hu hu hee, it is Hoksila. He is here.) Wana wichichala ke glopi kte kshto, hu hu hee, (All the girls will go home now, hu hu hee.)."

Hoksila smiled. This last bird was a female and she was very talkative. The Waki-yela is a female too. He couldn't help laughing.

Hoksila told the meadowlarks his plans. They agreed. Yes, the spotted red buffalo had a whole herd for his family. Yes, the birds knew Hoksila was here, but they did not know where. They told him the maidens were still along the lake. But the spotted red buffalo had guards and scouts everywhere now. How will Hoksila manage to get a message to his wife?

Hoksila pulled out some Sinkpuy-tawoti and chewed one. Then he took a few strands of his hair. These he cut off with his big hunting knife. He picked up his friend the waki-yela and spoke to it. "Ho Waki-yela, toku wan lela wachi yelo, (Ho turtledove, there is something I really want). Go to my wife and tell her to expect me. I am here. The meadowlark will guide you to me. Tell her this. Do not be afraid, she is waiting."

The waiting meadowlark was very anxious. Just like a female she was very impatient to leave, chirping out, "She, huwa. Wana unye kte kshto, enakni na, (Let's go now, yes, we are going now.)"

Hoksila took the sage and rubbed himself thoroughly killing all man-smell. He took one of the special arrows and fitted it on his bow. The other two he stuck in his waist strap. Now he must get as close as he could to that little lake and find out all he could while there was still daylight.

Suddenly his scout came running back. The coyote scout stopped in front of him, then trotted in another direction. Hoksila sensed some-

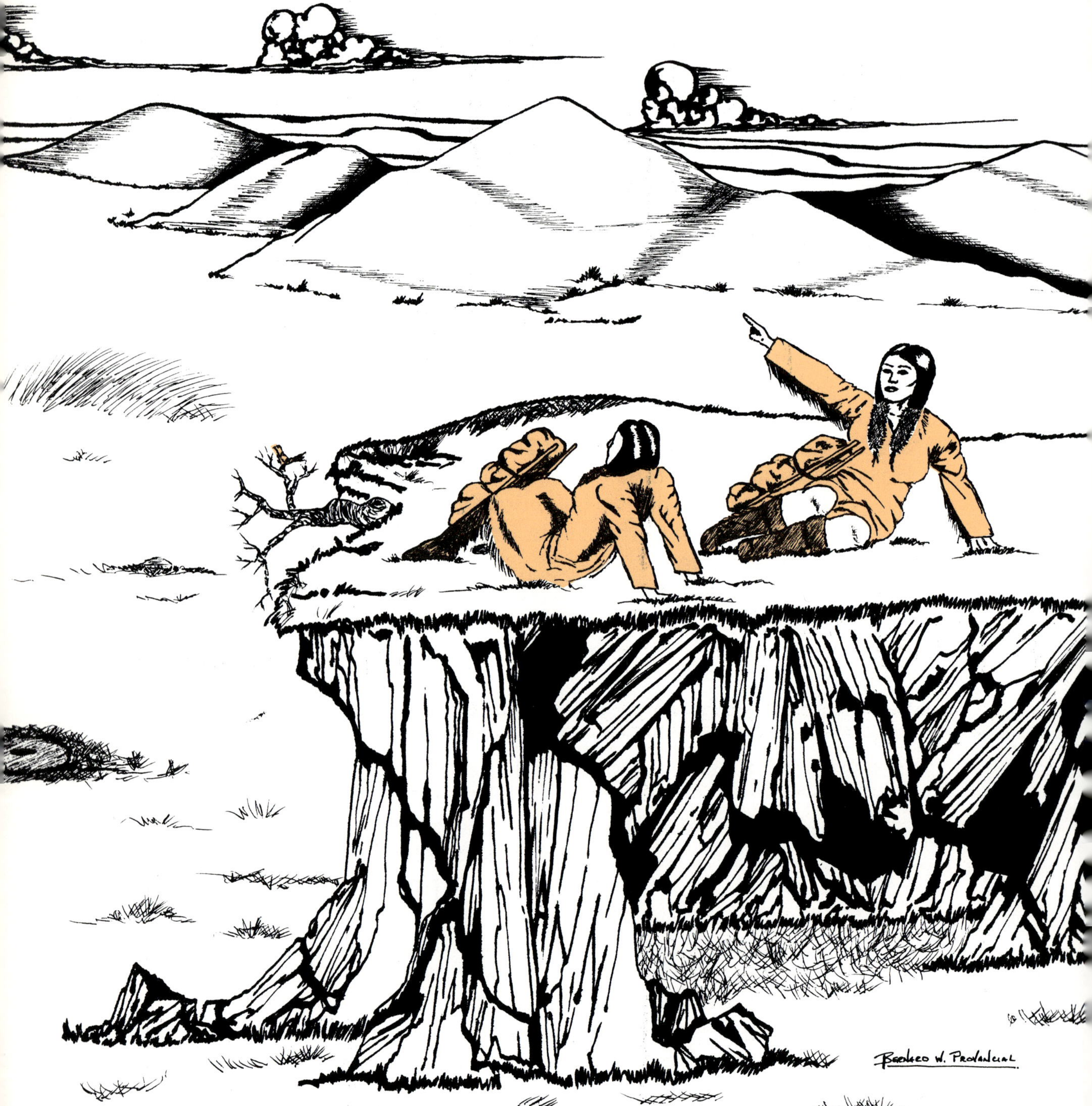

thing was wrong and followed his scout. They came to a gully and the coyote crawled in. Hoksila followed. Soon they heard the deep rumbling throaty growl of a buffalo bull. Hoksila was very anxious to see this red buffalo with the ugly black spots. He peeked over the tall weeds around the gully. But this was not that certain bull. It was a young bull though, probably out looking for Hoksila. There was one of those noisy magpies perched on the young bull's hump. Strangely, the bird was very quiet.

Along the shore of the lake below the twin peaks two beautiful young maidens were gathering wild onions. They had been there for a long time. Pejuta-washti-win (Good-Medicinewoman) is from one of the villages the spotted red buffalo raided. Her companion and friend, Tokcha-ska-win (White-deer Woman) was from a village further north. Pejuta-washti-win sat down and talked to her friend.

"That warrior from the thundercloud told us my husband was coming to free us. I wonder where he is at this time. Is he close or is he here now?" She asked this mostly to herself. Tokcha-ska-win answered, "Maybe he is watching us now. All the pte (buffalo) are worried about something. The whole herd has moved in very close to us. I wonder why."

As they sat and talked a meadowlark flew in close and landed. It walked over close and announced, "Hoksila wana he kshto, (Hoksila is here now.)."

Pejuta-Washti-win came over to Tokcha-ska-win and said, "I think I understand that bird. It's saying that my husband is here. It talks like a woman."

"I understand her, too," answered Tokcha-ska-win. "The message was very plain. And look over here!"

A little turtledove was fly-hopping in short stretches coming closer all the time. Soon the waki-yela stopped hopping and just walked to meet them, tired from all its fly-hopping.

In the brush close to the stream he found some abandoned duck's nests and some feathers. The turtledove flew to a tree branch and looked while Hoksila gathered everything he needed. Now he could make the right kind of arrows. The choice sticks he pulled from the beaver's water dam were just as he hoped. They were straight and waterlogged. They would make strong heavy straight arrows.

The sun was still very high so he picked a shady spot, sat down and started making his arrows. The turtledove was staying close making short flights. It was getting stronger with every try. Suddenly the Shung-monitu let out some low growls and started pulling on Hoksila's moccasins. Alarm was in the air. It was too late. They heard the yakking cackle of the unkchi-kika, (magpie). The spotted red buffalo's spy had seen them. Hoksila had an arrow notched fast. He let it fly but the noisy unkchi-kika glided away and out of sight. The news of Hoksila's arrival would be known before the sun sank to the horizon.

There was no need to hide anymore. It was now time to outsmart the crafty red buffalo in his own territory. This was going to be a hard thing to do. Hoksila ran up a rise to see which way the bird flew. The twin peaks were very visible from there. He remembered the lake somewhere below them. He tried to remember everything he was told. Still something was wrong. He looked closely at the twin peaks. He must go there now. He still had some time left before sunset. He walked slowly back to the shade of the tree he had rested under. He had to do some good thinking. His presence was now known and that was bad. As he sat, the waki-yela flew back to him. It was getting stronger all the time. As he thought, he was looking at the bird walking around in front of him.

He must let his wife know he had come after her and he was going to free all the other young maidens. Suddenly he laughed and picked up the bird. The great Tunkasila just told him what he must do. He called his guide the Shung-monitu to talk to him.

"Ho Kola Moshli, if we wait much longer that beast and his whole family will start looking for us and find us. We must hurry. There is a lake a little distance from those peaks. The maidens we seek are there. My wife is expecting me and she is waiting. I must tell her I am here so she will be prepared to leave."

The maidens quickly ran up and sat down in the path in front of the walking bird. They sat down facing each other, each watching to her front and left. An old warrior trick, they were scouting the entire area at the same time. The Waki-yela walked up to them, stopped and cooed. Pejuta-Washti-win (Good-medicine-woman) picked up the bird and inspected it. She was silently crying as she handed the bird to Tokcha-ska-win (White-deer-woman). The message was plain indeed.

Pejuta-washti-win's husband was here and they were going to be free. The bird had brought the chewed end of Sinkpay-tawoti and it was still wet. The hair the bird brought told them who it was from. Both maidens silently cried in joy. They were going to be free and so were all the other captive maidens. The maidens had a communication system amongst them that only they could understand. The two maidens must now tell the others to get ready.

They were all aware that it would be a difficult, possibly long struggle before they could actually be free and out of danger. They all knew that the terrible red bull with the ugly black spots should be killed. The thunder warrior that had come to Pejuta-washti-win had told her the news of her husband's becoming a man and coming to kill the buffalo who kept her captive.

Among the young maidens there was a popular little maiden. She was popular because she liked to sing so all the maidens caressingly called her the "Tio-shlo-win" (Cricket). They all listened when she sang. Her songs were of their forefathers, their warrior fathers and brothers. She told of the buffalo hunts and the wars and made them forget a lot of their troubles with her sweet voice. She was a gift to these young maidens in captivity. Now she was going to sing them the best song they had ever heard. It would be her last song along this lake. They were leaving. Pejuta-washti-win and Tokcha-ska-win gathered all the wild onions they picked and brought them among the groups of young maidens along the shore. They approached Tio-shlo-win and a group of maidens preparing some food. They showed them the Waki-yela and the message. The group of maidens became excited and spread the news. It was only a matter of time and all the maidens knew of the plan.

They would cook an evening meal and after this meal Tio-shlo would sing for them again. She would tell them the whole plan in her song and the buffalo would not know. This was the day they all had been waiting for.

Hoksila and Shung-monitu waited long after the buffalo and the Unkchay-kika passed before they came out of the gully and resumed their journey. They ran in a long draw that finally turned. They came out to check their position with the twin peaks. They crawled to the top of a low hill. Hoksila was surprised as was Shung-monitu, to see how close they were to the lake and the twin peaks. But, something was wrong. They could make out the maidens in the distance. A big spotted red buffalo was lounging on a knoll above them. Suddenly Hoksila held his head and pressed himself to the ground. Now he knew what was wrong. He almost cried as he realized this. And he was so close to completing his intended work to free his wife and the maidens.

The Shung-monitu saw Hoksila's distress and came over to him. The warrior put his hand on the coyote's head and said, "Kola, that peak with the big rock ledge is supposed to be on my right. But, it is on my left. We must go back, go around those peaks and come in from the other side or the rescue will not work."

The boy warrior dropped his hand from the coyote's head and lay very still. He was thinking. Finally he said, "Kola, those scouts are looking for us everywhere. We are not safe anywhere. But we will go back, track that buffalo and follow it. I'm sure it will scout to the other side of those peaks. The buffalo cannot see that far, but it can smell us. All they will smell will be sage. We must get on the other side of those peaks and we must do so quickly."

Hoksila slid backwards until he was back in the draw. He got up and ran back to that certain gully. He went over and looked for tracks. Finding them he called, "Shung-monitu, hu wo letchiya, (Coyote, come over here)." When the coyote came over he pressed its nose on the tracks. "Ho Kola, pte ki oyuspa yo, (Ho friend, catch this buffalo.)" The coyote, with its nose close to the ground, started out at a run. Hoksila called to the male meadowlark as he started running after the now fast-moving coyote. From here Hoksila could see the twin peaks. Soon they were directly to his left. He was glad the buffalo they were tracking was moving fast. Soon they were moving toward the peaks.

Hoksila couldn't help smiling. The sun was sending its last hottest rays. It was nearing its last horizon. Then that maiden would spread her black shawl over the land so all could rest. Suddenly Hoksila did not want this. He wished the sun would stay up forever. He had too much to do. He badly wanted to talk to his wife and her friends. Mostly he wanted to meet this spotted red buffalo.

Slowly the peak was turning into two again; that meant they were getting behind them. It was time to head for that rock ledge. Now it would be on his right. Just then they caught up to the buffalo and that noisy Unkchay-kika. Hoksila was in a hurry—the sun was going down.

That buffalo could not see them but that Unkchay-kika could. Hoksila had a plan and they headed straight for the buffalo.

Soon they came to a long draw that led into the sunset. Hoksila and the coyote went into it and were soon ahead of the buffalo and the bird. It was time to stop and rest and make their next plans. After getting their breath they resumed their running until they came to a bend that led them directly in front of the buffalo coming at a fast walk. When the buffalo got close the coyote came out but stayed within arrow range of Hoksila. It laid down and played dead. With feet thrust out and head thrown back it looked like a long-dead coyote, a delicious target for any magpie. Soon, the buffalo paced by but stayed at a distance. The nosey magpie spotted the ''dead'' coyote. Immediately it left the buffalo to check out this delicious meal and nest of fleas. It flew high, first to see if there was anything else nearby. Hoksila was well-concealed so he was not spotted. Seeing all was clear, the Unkchay-kika landed on the ''dead'' coyote. Before the bird realized it was fooled an arrow was swishing through the air. It came from a very strong bow. The arrow point was sharp and fine. It passed through the bird in its mouth and ran back into the draw.

Hoksila waited until his coyote finished his meal of fresh meat, then they proceeded toward the peaks. Staying in the draws and gullies, they soon reached the bottom of the peaks. Hoksila carefully selected the one with the large rock ledge before he started his climb. The ever-alert Shung-monitu was always in front of him his protective scout, gift of the thunder warrior.

The steep hillside was almost barren. The only cover they had was the abundance of sandcherry bushes, but these were only as high as Hoksila's leggings. For no reason at all Hoksila stopped, picked some sandcherries and ate them. His Grandmother had told him that if he came upwind to these cherries they were sweet. If one came downwind they were bitter. The cherries were sweet. He smiled and moved on. They were almost to the ledge where rock-gardens and outcroppings were plentiful. They met little lizards scampering everywhere. The coyote ran ahead to see what was scaring these little creatures. Hoksila ran after him to keep up. As he ran, he stepped on a rock that turned. Losing his balance he fell to the ground.

He landed right in front of a snake laying in a sand patch just waiting for him. The snake stiffened the entire length of its body, ready to spring. In the blink of an eye it could coil and strike. These snakes were lightning fast. One of the little lizards close to Hoksila raised its head and front legs, stretching itself fully to its short length. Then, in a blur, it ran past the snake's head all the way to the tip of its tail. Turning in a blink, the little lizard jumped off, looked at Hoksila, and let out a high, shrill giggle like a whistle. Then, it ran off into the sandcherry bushes. Hoksila recovered, retrieved his bow, and struck the snake, then turned it over. It was very limp and very dead.

"Ho Hoksila, inaji yo, (Ho Hoksila, stand up!)!" The Thunder Warrior was here. Was it for the last time? The meadowlark was sitting on his shoulder and the Shung-Monitu was already here. The meadowlark (Tashia-Gnupa) said, "Ho-hee Hoksila, wana k'ela kshto, (Ho-hee Hoksila, it is close now.) Oni le pi kshto, (They are looking for you.) Wokta ichu na, (Be careful!)!"

The meadowlark was a female and she was very concerned and worried. The Thunder Warrior had a foot on a rock and leaning on one knee as he spoke said, "You have done well Hoksila. Maybe too fast. Your enemy knows you are here. His whole family is out looking for you. The ledge is the only place they will overlook in their hunt for you. But, in the daylight you are in constant danger. Are you afraid to fight in the dark?"

Hoksila answered, "There is a moon out tonight. If I can see the beast I will slay it. I want to free my wife and all the captive maidens. Also, I need the buffalo's hide to make a good tipi for my dear Grandmother."

Saying this he picked up the dead snake and looked at it. It was completely smashed. The Thunder Warrior spoke on, "I am glad to know that. You will need help to free the maidens at night. The fire-fly lives by night so it will help you. Also, it will mark your target well when you go to slay the red buffalo with the big ugly black spots. You will not miss. Your other helper is the cricket. They will call to each other like the cricket. Also, the insect knows how to hide. When the time comes you will listen for the cricket. That's where the maidens will be. Your last helper is the owl who sees at night. It will tell the maidens which way to go and where."

The Thunder Warrior checked Hoksila's arrows and said, "Now I will tell your wife all this. When the owl hoots in the night, you will be coming to slay the beast. When the cricket chirps the maidens will answer, gather together and go to the sound. The firefly will mark the path for them. When the owl hoots again, they must go straight to the hoot. They will stay together with the chirp sounds and the fire-fly will mark their way.

"When the sun sets and the moon is high you will go in and carry out your vow. You have courage and love for a wife you have never seen. Be brave. She will be waiting for you. Hoka hai!" The Thunder Warrior finished. Hoksila answered, "Hoka hai!", then he turned and looked at the coyote and scout just now returning. He was not surprised to see the warrior was gone when he looked again. He wondered if he could ever be one of them. He silently fell behind his scout and they headed for the huge rock ledge. They finally got to it and Hoksila laid flat on his stomach as not to be seen by the Unkchay-kika or anything else. It seemed like the ledge was above the whole country side. Hoksila could see everything in plain sight. The lake, the groups of maidens, and all along the shores were clear. He checked every draw and gully leading to the lake. He needed every one of them.

Pejuta-washtay-win and Tokcha-ska-win sat inspecting the Waki-yela when the Thunder Warrior spoke to them, "I see your husband has already told you he has come after you. That is good."

The maidens looked up in surprise. The Meadowlark on the War-rior's shoulder spoke on, "Wana yaglopi kte kshto, iglu wiyiya pe, (You will be going home now so start preparing.)." The Warrior and the maidens laughed as the meadowlark looked at them closely with a cocked head and said, "Mni ota u hapi, tehunta kshto, (Carry lots of water. You have a long way.)." The female meadowlark just loved to give advice or just talk to the maidens. She was very concerned.

Pejuta-washtay-win asked, "Is my husband tall and handsome? He seems very brave to come after me all alone."

The Thunder Warrior answered, "He was raised by his grand-mother to do what he is doing. He has no mother or father. All he has is a grandmother. He wants the spotted red buffalo's hide to make her a tipi. Tonight he will be here.

"I must now prepare you for your escape and the long journey to your homes. The Warriors of the Four Winds will help Hoksila. His grandmother fasted and prayed for this. Now this is what you must do."

"Wait!" cried Tokcha-ska-win, "I will get Tio-shlo-win. She can tell all the maidens what they must do. They listen to every word she sings."

Tio-shlo-win was quickly brought to the warrior. She stood wide-eyed staring at the warrior but listened to every word she was told. She had tears in her eyes as she told the warrior, "This is the greatest honor in my whole life. I am called Tio-shlo-win because I like to sing. I am named after the Wablushka-tio-shlo (insect that chirps in the dwelling). I am so happy that my namesake will be helping us. We will remember this for the rest of our lives. We will tell our children—you will be remembered forever." She finished with a big smile wiping the tears from her cheeks.

After all this the warrior turned to Pejuta-washtay-win and said, "The Waki-yela was saved by your husband. A big snake ate her eggs and tried to eat her too. Your husband killed the snake and is using its hide to tie his hair. The Waki-yela has given your husband three beautiful wishes that she will grant instantly as she has magic and charm. Take three fluffed feathers from her breast. Give these to Hoksila. When he is in a position where he needs help very badly tell him to throw a fluff in the air and make a wish. The wish will come true instantly."

The Warrior told Pejuta-washtay-win that her husband must do this only when he needed help. Then the Warrior said, "Tell your sisters to ask the Warriors of the Four Winds to give Hoksila strength and courage. If he wins this battle, you will be free and you can go home. Ask the invisible Warriors to help him for you. Hoka hai!" The maidens watched the thunder warrior and the Tashia-gnupa fade away.

The sun was slowly sliding behind the horizon. The maidens had eaten a hearty meal. Small fires were built and the maidens sat listening to Tio-shlo-win sing her evening songs. She walked slowly through the many small campfire circles singing her songs. Suddenly the big red bull with the ugly black spots threw a rage. It started bellowing and growling as it stood on the hill pawing grass and dirt in the air. A small dust cloud rose from all this sudden rampaging. Soon all the other bulls joined him and the whole herd of buffalo started forming a circle around the lake. The spotted red bull was still on the hill raging on. Everything was a dust haze as the sun sank behind the hills. The great bull kept up its rampaging. Soon the moon was out and rising in the night skies. All around the lake it was noisy as all the bulls bellowed, pawed dirt in the air and were looking for something.

Suddenly all was quiet. The moon was high. All the little fires the maidens had going were put out. Just the spotted red bull's angry low growling and throaty rumblings were heard. Then there was the sound of a coyote barking at the far end of the lake. The maidens were waiting for an owl's hooting. Suddenly the coyote's barking turned to howling and growling as it attacked the buffalo. The entire lake area came alive as the other buffalo ran to aid the one being attacked.

The spotted red buffalo remained on the hill. An owl hooted in one of the draws. Hoksila? In the moonlight everything was in plain sight. Little crickets started chirping just below the still raging spotted red bull. The maidens started imitating the chirping. They gathered in groups and started toward the sound. They could feel the fireflies landing on their cheeks. The red buffalo with the ugly black spots sensed something was going to happen. Pawing dirt and bellowing it came off the knoll and attacked the maidens who were now gathered in groups headed toward him. Tio-shlo-win was leading the maidens. The maidens watched the red beast coming to attack them but they kept going their pace, chirping like the Cricket, even as the red beast was coming to attack them.

Suddenly they heard a man yell, ''Hoka hai Tatunka Gleshka, wana wahi yelo, (Hoka hai spotted buffalo, I am here now.). Chikte naha ha netawa ki un Unjiji tipi waji wechoki kte lo, (I am going to kill you and make a tipi for my Grandmother with your hide.) Between them now, a lone figure rose and raised both hands in the air. He proclaimed this battle his alone. He notched an arrow on his bow and knelt. The bellowing raging bull never slowed down. It was too angry. Hoksila knelt and took aim with his first arrow on a glittering patch on the charging red buffalo. He let the arrow fly. The buffalo never even noticed it. He notched his second arrow and waited. He felt the thundering of the beast's hooves on the ground where he knelt. He could see its horns when he let the arrow fly. Then he felt and smelled the red beast as it slammed into him, knocking him high in the air. He landed on his feet. Pulling out his big bone hunting knife, he jumped on the beast's head and started stabbing it.

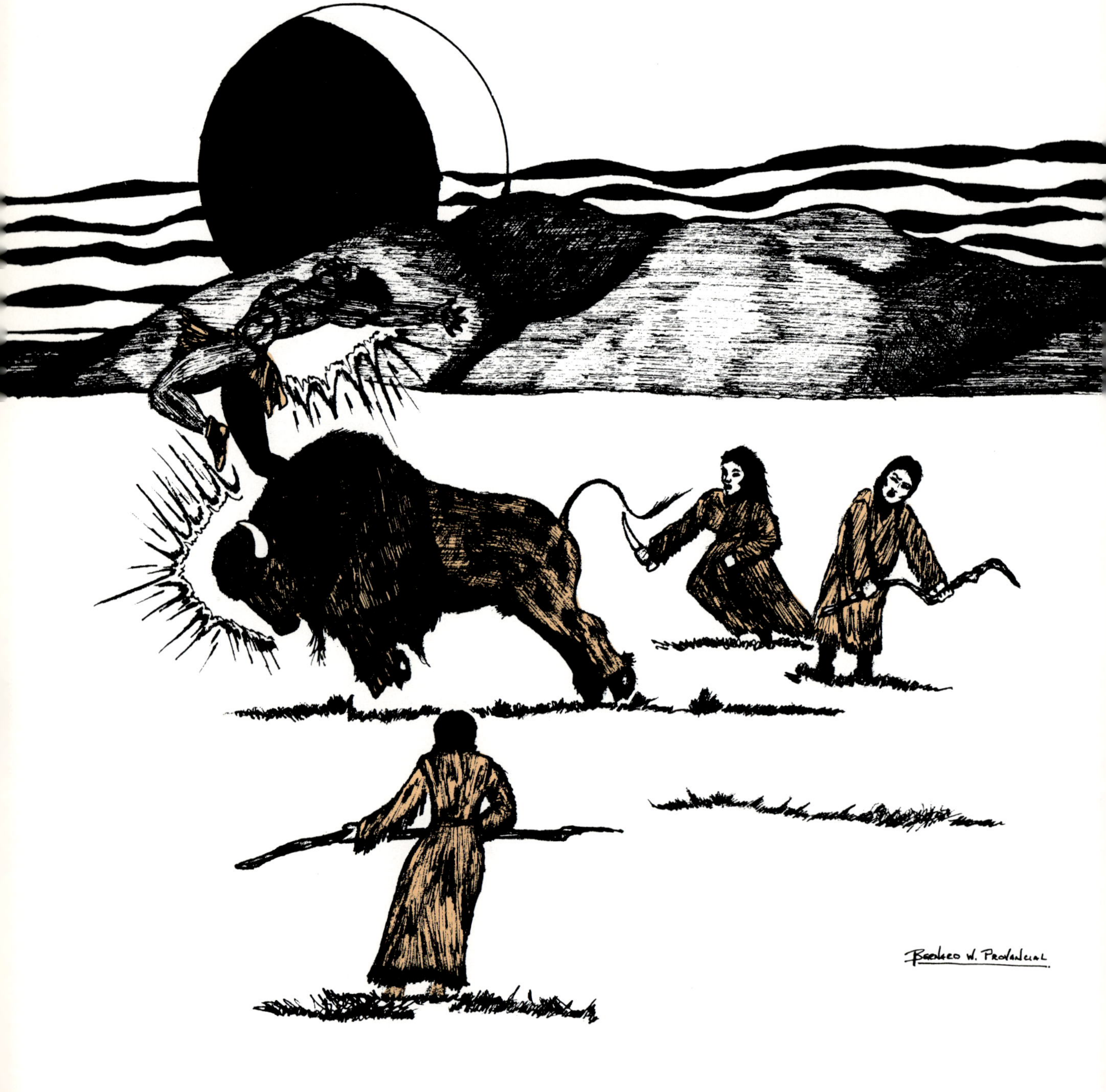

By then all the maidens were there. One of them came first and threw her arms around his neck. "Hoksila ney hai, (Are you Hoksila?)" she yelled. "Hoka hai," answered Hoksila. The maiden yelled, "You are my husband!"

They had to yell to each other as all of a sudden the noise had become deafening. Hoksila's big bone knife had been taken from him. All the maidens with their own makeshift weapons were happily skinning the red buffalo with the big ugly black spots. Hoksila couldn't figure out who had killed the beast. Was it his two arrows or all the maidens with their bare hands and makeshift weapons? Their years of captivity had made them hate this beast passionately.

Time seemed to pass very fast. Soon the red buffalo was skinned and the maidens were ready to start their long journey to their homes. Pejuta-washtay-win made it clear to Hoksila that her place was beside him from now on. A group of the maidens from Hoksila's own village wanted to take the red buffalo's hide to his grandmother and tell her everything that had happened.

Now the morning star was coming into view. The maidens must hurry. The trail marked by the fireflies would be gone. Hoksila and his wife remained until the last. By then it was dawn. The owl would lead the maidens to safety, Hoksila was sure of that. Just then, the Unkchay-kika cackled. The bird saw them from where it was lying in the dirt. In the sudden rush of dawn the maidens had forgotten to hide the huge head of the dead spotted beast.

The Unkchay-kika saw the head and knew what had happened. Hoksila notched an arrow and shot at the bird, but the bird dodged and the arrow flew away. Now it was too late. It was taking the news to the buffalo herd. All the maidens and Hoksila knew they would be attacked by the herd. Hoksila thought for a moment. Now he must lead the buffalo herd away from the maidens who had just found their freedom.

Pejuta-washtay-win ran after Tokcha-ska-win who was awaiting her. The two beautiful young maidens faced each other solemnly knowing this would be their last meeting. Tokcha-ska-win would take the hide of the big spotted red buffalo straight to the lodge of Hoksila's Grandmother where she would tell the women of her grandson's great deed, how he destroyed the fearsome beast and freed all the captive maidens. This was what Hoksila's Grandmother had prayed and fasted for. Now the great deed was done and her prayers were answered.

Hoksila tried very hard to make Pejuta-washtay-win go with Tokcha-ska-win but to no avail. His wife was very stubborn. "Many years I waited. I will never cry or be lonesome again," she said. With that she would not listen to anybody anymore.

Tio-shlo-win ran back to them to see what was going on and heard everything. She enjoined, "We will return to our homes and tell everything Hoksila has done. He will be given a warrior's name and be remembered forever." She asked, "What are you going to do now?"

Hoksila answered, "The noisy Unkchay-kika has seen what I've done. He will go back to the beast's family and tell everything. Now you must follow the owl who will lead you to safety. Then, go home from there. Be sure and do just that. Now I must wait for my Shung-monitu scout to return so we can lead the herd away from you when they attack."

Tio-shlo-win said, "I will lead the maidens to safety. Then I will follow the owl. I will go now." She started to leave.

Just then they heard thunder and lightning strike. The Thunder Warrior stood before them once more. The meadowlark was not on his shoulder. Instead he held it tenderly in his hand cupped to his chest. "I had to return," the warrior said, "And I see that Hoksila has made a wish come true for his grandmother. She raised him with the prayer that he would do this. It is done. Now I must tell you the other. The Shung-monitu, the Moshli . . . that one will be with you no more. It was this past night. Our friend the owl told him the time to free the maidens was near but the pte (buffalo) were all around the lake. The maidens were still trapped so the Shung-monitu, the Moshli, attacked the bulls on the far end of the lake.

"Every buffalo went after him and he was surrounded by the herd. Now he is no more. From this day on the Tashia-gnupa vowed to wear a black necklace in memory of the Shung-monitu who was slain so the captive maidens could be free. Now the Unkchay-kika that got away has gone to the herd and told everything that has been done. The whole herd is raging angry and has vowed to destroy Hoksila and all the maidens."

The Thunder Warrior looked at the maidens and said, "There is not much time until daylight, then the buffalo can see or smell your trail. Hoksila will stay and lead the buffalo away from you. You must reach your homes where your own warriors will defend you. There is no more red buffalo with the big ugly black spots to be afraid of. You must leave now.''

Pejuta-washtay-win ran to Hoksila and held him. ''This is the farthest I will ever be from my husband from now on. If the terrible pte do to him what they did to his Shung-monitu I will want to be with them. I will never cry of lonesomeness for him again.'' Saying this she pulled out the three fluffed feathers the Waki-yela had given her and said, ''We will live to see our children grow. Tell this to the Hoksila's grandmother. She chose me for him, Pela maya (Thank you.).''

Just then they heard the distant rumble of what could only be a great buffalo stampede. The Thunder Warrior bent reaching into the grass and pulled out the already chopped-off tail of the spotted red buffalo. Giving it to Hoksila he told him, ''Take this and go back to the twin peaks. Make sure they see you. One of your Shung-monitu's grown pups will meet you there and guide you. From there go to the Eto-gaka (south). The herd will think the maidens are with you. This Tashia-gnupa will help all the maidens from here. Go now! Earn a name!''

Hoksila took the red buffalo's tail with the black tip and ran back toward the peaks. Pejuta-washtay-win ran right beside him and told him, ''I can run like a deer and am very good medicine for you. What is my name?'' She held his hand.

Despite being desperate and running hard, Hoksila blushed deeply. No maiden had ever held his hand before. His grandmother had held his hand but he was a mere child then.

The tip of the sun was now showing on the horizon. Hoksila got below the twin peaks and stood on the knoll waving the buffalo's tail and singing: *Ehuni Letchamu Kta Cha-oyag washi kun-toki oyaki sne ye-laka ya.* ''Long ago I said I was going to do this, I guess they didn't tell.'' AH HEY YO HEY YO HIYA HAYA HIYA HAYA.

Some Unkchay-kika saw and heard this. Some scouting buffalo heard it. They saw a maiden with Hoksila. Word quickly got back to the herd. The news was the Hoksila and all the maidens were back under the twin peaks. These were the ones who had tricked their beloved leader, the red buffalo with the big ugly black spots. Yes, they had used trickery to destroy him. This was the message the Unkchay-kika gave the buffalo herd.

A coyote howled along the lake. Hoksila and Pejuta-washtay-win came off the hill and ran toward it. Meeting the young coyote they followed it around the lake. Then they went to the Eto-gaka (south) and on through the hills. Now the angry buffalo herd knew where Hoksila and Pejuta-washtay-win were. After much running the Shung-monitu led Hoksila and Pejuta-washtay-win to a hilltop where they had a plain view of the buffalo herd. Suddenly they felt the ground shaking and heard the rumbling of hooves. The great buffalo were on the stampede. As they stood on the hill all they could see were dusty brown clouds as the buffalo herd came on to attack Hoksila. It was a great herd and Hoksila and Pejuta-washtay-win with their scout, the Shung-monitu, were trapped in the middle. There was no place to go, so the three stayed together on the hill. Soon the buffalo stampede was right up to them. The ground shook and rumbled.

Pejuta-washtay-win pulled out a fluffled feather of the Waki-yela and put it in Hoksila's hand. "We must raise a family of our own. Do what you must do," she told him.

Hoksila had the fluffed feather in the palm of his hand. He threw it up in the air and cried out, "Ho Tunkasila naha Waki-yela, (Ho grandfather and the turtledove,) Uni unchipi yelo, (We want to live.)."

Suddenly a wall of stones went up around Hoksila, his wife, and their coyote scout. The stampeding buffalo herd, blind to any obstacle in their rage, ran into the wall running with all their might. Inside the stone wall the three occupants sat and rested. They had been doing a lot of running. The ground and the wall shook every time the buffalo attacked. But the wall was too strong for the raging creatures. A lot of the buffalo laid still after they hit the wall. The Unkchay-kika lost their sense of loyalty to the buffalo and began to feed on those creatures which were dead. The stone wall was there to stay.

After a lull in the buffalo attacks there came three meadowlarks who took rest from their flight and sat on the wall. "Ho-hee oko ke kshto, (Ho-hee, there has been a lot of action)," exclaimed a bird. They were all females. They looked over the place from their vantage point on the stones and one said, "Tokay Hoksila, hokshichala cha enya wahokpi mahel yunkay se, (Hoksila looks like a baby in a rock nest.)." They all chuckled, "Tu-kee, hetcha kshto, enya hokshi hetcha kshto, (Tu-kee, that's what he is, he is a stone child)." They all shook their heads.

It was the third morning after the maidens were given their freedom and the spotted red buffalo slain that the Tashi-gnupa told the news in their early morning talk.

The maidens soon realized that what the "Enya-Hokshi" (the birds) were talking about was their hero, the one who had fought for their freedom. One of them was now his wife. So, on the evening the maidens were freed most of them entered their home villages. They all told a fantastic tale of a lone warrior named "Enya-Hokshi" who fought the most dreaded beast and easily put an end to him. All this, according to every maiden, became the "Enya-Hokshi" legend.

Hoksila, who didn't know his new name yet, hunted and fought the avenging buffalo daily. He must keep their attention away from his grandmother, the young people and the rest of the Lakota nation. Even in the years his own family was becoming many he still hunted and fought the buffalo children of that big red buffalo with the ugly black spots.

It was a long time after when two maidens sat with their children on a hill-top and talked. They had just visited an old woman who lived in a large, beautiful and strong tipi. The one named Tokcha-ska-win (White-deer-woman) pointed to some dusty low-blowing clouds and said, "Aki tatanka ki Enya-hokshi tokpopi," (The buffalo are attacking the Stone Child again). Woblushka-tio-shlo-win, taking her baby away from her breast answered, "Yes, he is still fighting them for us. Yes, and for our children." She chuckled and said, "I knew I would hear some news today because the crickets were talking in our tipi last night." Just then Enya-Hokshi's grandmother came up and sat down with them. Pointing to the low-blowing clouds she said, "Takoja, (grandchildren) the sign of my beloved Takoja fighting the children of the spotted red buffalo so the young people will be safe and happy. I knew something good would happen to me because some fireflies landed on my face last night."

Tokcha-ska-win talked, "It seems that when the crickets talk in our tipi we hear good news. When a firefly lands on us something good happens to us."

Wablushka-tio-shlo-win said, "My husband and a band were out hunting the other day. They saw a young Shung-monitu out hunting in the daylight—unusual. Then they knew it was scouting for Enya-hokshi. So, he took his hunters another way. On their way back they heard the Waki-yela (turtledove) crooning somewhere out on the prairie. They knew Enya-Hokshi's children were hiding nearby."

"Yes," answered Tokcha-ska-win, "The Waki-yela watches the children very close. I hear they are very mischievous and will get into trouble. She sings to them so they will behave or go to sleep." They all laughed at this.

Somewhere, someplace, sometime, out on that open country, another battle will take place. You can only tell by the scouting coyote and a turtle dove singing to the hiding children of Enya-Hokshi what is happening. When you see brown, dusty, low-blowing clouds you can say, "Aki Tatanka ki Enya-Hokshi tokpopi."

The buffalo are attacking the Stone-child again.